Protecting the Planet

ENVIRONMENTAL ACTIVISM

by Pamela Dell

Content Adviser: Roberta M. Johnson, Ph.D.,
Director, Education and Outreach,
University Corporation for Atmospheric Research, Boulder, Colorado

Science Adviser: Terrence E. Young Jr., M.Ed., M.L.S.,
Jefferson Parish (Louisiana) Public School System

Reading Adviser: Alexa L. Sandmann, Ed.D., Professor of Literacy,
College and Graduate School of Education, Health, and Human Services,
Kent State University

Compass Point Books
151 Good Counsel Drive
P.O. Box 669
Mankato, MN 56002-0669

This book was manufactured with paper containing
at least 10 percent post-consumer waste.

Photographs © Alamy: Mike Hill 8; AP Images: EyePress/File 15; Art Life Images: age fotostock/Sergio
Ferraris 16; Capstone Press: Karon Dubke 19 (all), 52; Corbis: Neil Rabinowitz 44, Peter Turnley 22,
Royalty-free/Tim Pannell 60; DigitalVision: 7, 47; Getty Images: Hulton Archive 13, Martin H. Simon-Pool
42, National Geographic/Michael Melford 39, Riser/David Woodfall 21, Visuals Unlimited/Wally Eberhart
33(b); iStockphoto: BirdImages 54, GlobalP 51, Jusant 11, MCCAIG 17, mikered 29, Thornberry 33(t);
Minden Pictures: Gerry Ellis 38; NASA: JPL 5; Shutterstock: Anna Kaminska 6(b), Arvydas Kniuksta
31, Avalon Imaging 32, Brian A. Jackson 58, Chris Burt 57, Chris Kruger 46, Evok20 28, forest badger 24,
Frontpage 53, gary yim 36–37, imageshunter 26, Joe Mercier 50, Mark William Richardson 10, maxstock-
photo 4, 14, 20, 30, 35, 45, 56, Sascha Burkard 6(t).

Editor: Jennifer VanVoorst
Designer: Heidi Thompson
Media Researcher: Wanda Winch
Art Director: LuAnn Ascheman-Adams
Creative Director: Joe Ewest
Editorial Director: Nick Healy
Managing Editor: Catherine Neitge

Library of Congress Cataloging-in-Publication Data
Dell, Pamela.
  Protecting the planet: environmental activism / by Pamela Dell.
    p. cm. — (Green generation)
  Includes index.
  ISBN 978-0-7565-4248-1 (library binding)
  ISBN 978-0-7565-4295-5 (paperback)
  1. Environmentalism—Juvenile literature.
  I. Title. II. Series.
  GE195.5.D45 2010
  333.72—dc22   2009008782

Visit Compass Point Books on the Internet at *www.compasspointbooks.com*
or e-mail your request to *custserv@compasspointbooks.com*

Contents

"You see that pale blue dot? That's us. Everything that has ever happened in all of human history has happened on that pixel. All the triumphs and all the tragedies, all the wars, all the famines, all the major advances. ... It's our only home. And that is what is at stake, our ability to live on planet Earth, to have a future as a civilization. I believe ... it is our time to rise again to secure our future."

–Al Gore, environmental activist, Nobel Prize winner, and former vice president of the United States

Our Beautiful Blue Planet

introduction

One of the most famous photographs in the world was shot in December 1972. This photo, taken at a distance of 28,000 miles (45,000 kilometers) out in space by the *Apollo 17* astronauts, was one of the first color images of planet Earth.

The dramatic photograph gave people who viewed it a sense of awe. From this cosmic perspective, Earth looks like a beautiful blue marble.

The National Aeronautics and Space Administration began capturing even more images of our planet. In 2002 NASA produced what it called a "photolike mosaic" using four months of data. The resulting image, named *Blue Marble*, was the most accurately colored and detailed image of Earth's surface that had ever been available. Looking at it gives the viewer a deeper appreciation of this living sphere we call home.

The blue of the ocean, the windswept swirls of white clouds, the vast stretches of red or tan desert, and the green forestlands tell the story of a planet that is extraordinarily alive.

The first "blue marble" photograph, taken by *Apollo 17* astronauts in 1972, prompted public interest in conservation.

This precious "blue marble" is a miracle of life in a solar system of otherwise lifeless orbs. Do we appreciate this life-nurturing place? How often do we take the astronaut's eye view and really think about what an amazing thing our planet is?

Earth provides everything we need, not just to live but also to thrive. We breathe its air and drink its water. We eat food that grows in its soil and use its natural resources to make homes to shelter us and clothes to keep us warm. What happens to Earth affects us in every way. But human beings are not alone on this planet, and all living things are directly affected by changes that occur throughout our world. For the sake of all of Earth's living things, it makes sense to value and protect these resources that keep us alive.

Today there is a global call to pay more attention to this vibrant life, because it is being threatened on all sides. The crises are many: Global warming, freshwater loss, and the destruction of plants and animals that make up the world's diverse ecosystems are just a few of the problems the planet faces.

Climate fever: Global warming is the most significant threat to Earth as we know it. Our planet is warming up, and this threatens the health of the planet and all things that live on it. Scientists believe that the way we use our planet's resources has given Earth a fever. We burn fossil fuels, such as coal, oil, and natural gas, to create electricity, power vehicles, and heat and cool our homes. Burning these fuels emits vast amounts of carbon dioxide into the atmosphere. Carbon dioxide is a greenhouse gas. It and other gases create a blanket that traps the sun's heat close to Earth, much like the glass walls of a greenhouse. When

Global warming is causing polar ice to melt, affecting ocean levels worldwide.

large amounts of these gases are released, the atmosphere warms up too much. The heat threatens life-forms that have adapted to earlier climate conditions. Earth's temperature has been rising for some time, and we are beginning to see the dire effects.

As the planet heats up, ice caps melt, causing sea levels to rise and leading to flooding in coastal areas.

Scientists predict that global warming will cause major shifts in weather patterns, creating stronger hurricanes, heavier snowfalls, and more severe droughts. Global warming also threatens the habitats of millions of living things besides humans. Many plants and animals will not be able to adapt to changes, and many species—and some entire ecosystems—could be lost.

Hurricanes and other extreme weather are increasing in intensity because of rising global temperatures.

This could mean irreversible changes in the way we exist on Earth.

Some shocking statistics:

Compared with other living things, human beings have always exploited Earth's resources on a grand scale. But until the last century or so, our use of these resources had little effect. The damage to Earth was happening gradually. In recent decades, however, the situation has taken a dramatic turn for the worse. How much worse? Consider this: In only the last 35 years, people have used up an astounding one-third of Earth's natural resources. If we keep up this tremendous rate of consumption, will there be anything left in another 70 years?

The United States consumes—and wastes—far more than any other nation. The United States has just 5 percent of the world's population, yet its citizens create 30 percent of the world's waste and use 30 percent of the world's resources. Today only 4 percent of this country's original forests still exist. Forty percent of U.S. waterways are too polluted to drink from. American industries release 4 billion pounds (1.8 billion kilograms) of poisonous chemicals into the air every year. At least that's how much businesses admit to. The actual amount may be even greater.

Becoming globally green:

These are only a few of the facts, but they add up to an urgent situation. Fortunately global awareness of these problems has been rising. The United Nations has developed eight goals that it has challenged the world to accomplish by 2015. Called the Millennium

Development Goals, they range from ending world hunger to creating a partnership of nations that will cooperate on every level. One of the goals is called Environmental Sustainability. It focuses on reducing greenhouse gas emissions, preserving freshwater, preventing deforestation, and protecting wildlife. With high-profile celebrities such as U2 rock star Bono promoting the U.N.'s program, the goals get a lot of attention.

National governments are enacting and enforcing important laws to protect resources as well. In fact, in 2009, the U.S. Environmental Protection Agency declared carbon dioxide and five other greenhouse gases to be pollutants. This allowed federal regulation of the heat-trapping gases

The burning of fossil fuels by power plants is one of the primary causes of global warming.

for the first time in history. Three important U.S. laws to protect the environment are already on the books: the Clean Air Act, the Clean Water Act, and the Endangered Species Act.

On a nongovernmental level, much is going on, too. Governments make the laws, of course, but individual people get the ball rolling. Countless environmental groups and individual citizens are working worldwide. They are tackling the pressing environmental problems of our time, trying to meet the challenges caused by human consumption. These people and organizations are trying, in a wide variety of ways, to reverse the damage already done. Their efforts range from improving the quality of air and water to saving endangered plants and animals. They include developing safe, environmentally friendly sources of energy and promoting green living in all ways. It has never been more important to take care of the planet, and people everywhere are pitching in to "green up" their lives and life on Earth in general.

Future generations will inherit a world that is still strikingly alive and rich with resources—or they will not. You can become an environmental activist and get involved in making our planet a better place. It's all up to us and the actions we take, starting right now.

GO DEEP

Earth Day

On April 22, 1970, an event took place that, two decades later, *American Heritage* magazine called "one of the most remarkable happenings in the history of democracy." That event was the first-ever Earth Day. Since then, April 22 every year has been Earth Day.

Earth Day was the idea of U.S. Senator Gaylord Nelson of Wisconsin. He was upset about the negative effects of human activity on the air, land, and water. Although his concerns were shared by millions of people, Nelson noticed that two groups almost completely ignored the problems. These were America's political leaders and news media. Frustrated by this lack of attention, Nelson began trying to get some political and media focus on environmental problems. At a conference in the fall of 1969, Nelson announced that a nationwide public demonstration would protest the lack of governmental concern about the environment. Anyone who wanted to join the protest was welcome.

"The response was electric," Nelson later said. "It took off like gangbusters." This first "national day of observance of environmental problems," as *The New York Times* called it, was a big success. In cities and towns from coast to coast, about 20 million demonstrators showed up. People everywhere organized festivities of all kinds, including activities to clean up, beautify,

Kids in New York City celebrated the first Earth Day by cleaning up their neighborhoods.

or otherwise honor the planet.

Nelson said that once he had announced the event, "it organized itself." That was because thousands of passionate volunteers, most of them of college age, made sure it did. The attention Earth Day brought to important issues led directly to vital environmental protection laws, such as the Clean Air Act and Clean Water Act.

By 1990 Earth Day had spread to 141 countries and had as many as 200 million participants worldwide. By 2000 Earth Day activists around the world were linked by the Internet. In 2009 Earth Day was celebrated by more than 1 billion people.

"Oh beautiful for smoggy skies, insecticided grain. For strip-mined mountain's majesty above the asphalt plain. America, America, man sheds his waste on thee. And hides the pines with billboard signs, from sea to oily sea."
—George Carlin (1937–2008), comedian

The Air We Breathe

chapter 1

In 1684 a well-known English diarist named John Evelyn wrote that London's smog problem was so great that "hardly could one see across the street." Evelyn was not the only one disturbed by the situation. The complainers, though, were few and far between. Now, more than 300 years later, those voices have risen to a global chorus that won't be ignored. Much more aware of the dangers of pollution, people everywhere are cleaning up their act. Still, in most places, the air, water, and soil could use a lot of improvement.

Have you ever had one of those days when you looked outside and couldn't see the usual distant panorama— say the mountains or the city skyline? You knew they were there, but a brownish layer of smog was hiding them entirely. If you've never experienced a "bad air day," you're lucky. The lack of a good scenic view is a downside of air pollution, but there are much more serious consequences. Since each of us takes in an average of about 3,000 gallons (11,370 liters) of air every day, it's important for the air to be clean. Breathing dirty air every day can cause many physical and mental problems. Some of the most serious are asthma, brain damage, birth defects, and cancer. But air pollution doesn't just hurt humans and other animals. It can

China is particularly affected by pollution, and its citizens sometimes wear masks for protection.

damage crops, trees, and even bodies of water, such as lakes. Acid rain is one effect of air pollution that can have a disastrous impact on the environment. Burning coal gives off chemical particles that turn to acids when they mix with moisture in the air. Eventually the chemicals fall back to Earth as acid rain or snow. Acid rain can make the water of a lake so acidic that it kills organisms in the lake. On land acid rain can damage or kill trees and other plants.

Another problem with air pollutants is that some of them rise high into Earth's upper atmosphere. Their presence there thins the protective ozone layer. Without the ozone layer, the sun's rays stream down to Earth much more powerfully. With the blanket of greenhouse gases holding

Acid rain and snow destroys forests, makes water too acidic for life, and even breaks down stone.

warm air close to Earth's surface, the increased intensity of the sun's rays can cause the planet to heat up even more quickly.

The Clean Air Act:

Fortunately elected officials in the United States acknowledge the problems caused by air pollution and have passed legislation to address it. First enacted in 1970, the federal Clean Air Act includes guidelines for reducing toxic pollutants in the air and stopping the most common types of air pollution. The law also sets emission standards for cars, trucks, and other motorized vehicles and has guidelines for enforcing those standards. It contains information on dealing with air pollution carried into the United States from elsewhere, as well as guidelines for protecting the ozone

Tough new rules for U.S. vehicle emissions and mileage standards will begin to take effect in 2012.

layer. In 1990 the Clean Air Act was dramatically updated. The new, revised law is much tougher on those who create air pollution. State and local governments, as well as the governments of tribal nations, are also doing a lot to enforce the law and go after violators.

You can help! Those whose work is enforcing the Clean Air Act and dealing with air polluters are on the job every day. For everyone else, pollution can be an easy problem to forget, especially when there isn't enough smog to actually make the air visible. But that air may still be unhealthy to breathe. Here are some ways you and your family can help reduce the problem—whether you can see the pollution in the air or not.

- If you think you've found a source of air pollution, report it to the U.S. Environmental Protection Agency. This organization enforces laws that protect the environment.
- Motor vehicles are among the planet's biggest polluters. Walk, bike, or use public transportation, such as buses or trains, as much as possible.
- Report motor vehicles that are emitting a lot of tailpipe smoke.
- Conserve energy by turning off all appliances and lights when you leave a room. Most electricity is made by burning fossil fuels. This process releases pollutants, including the greenhouse gas carbon dioxide, into the atmosphere.
- Don't wait in long drive-through lines, letting the car engine idle. Idling wastes energy and needlessly pollutes the air.

Park and walk in!

- In cold weather, don't start your car long before you leave in order to warm up the inside. Just get in and drive off.

- Recycle glass, plastic, paper, aluminum cans, and cardboard. This reduces manufacturing emissions and saves energy, too.

- Plant a tree. Trees give off oxygen and take in carbon dioxide, helping remove one of the worst greenhouse gases from the environment.

Let your plastic bottle live again by recycling it. It might come back as a fleece jacket or a ballpoint pen.

"Water and air, the two essential fluids on which all life depends, have become global garbage cans. ... We forget that the water cycle and the life cycle are one."
    —Jacques Cousteau (1910–1997), marine explorer and conservationist

The Water We Drink

chapter 2

Benjamin Franklin supposedly said, "When the well runs dry, we shall know the value of water." Around the world, people everywhere take their water supply for granted. It rains, so there will always be more, right? Wrong.

Water is considered a renewable resource because the natural cycle of evaporation and condensation constantly circulates water, so that it is always new. But the amount of freshwater that people can use is shrinking. That's because global warming is causing Earth's water to be redistributed. Furthermore,

Treated water dumped into lakes and streams may not be entirely rid of environmental poisons.

the waste and pollution of freshwater are using up our supply faster than natural processes can make more of it. Some water is permanently polluted, so it can never be used. Some scientists consider the loss of freshwater the world's greatest environmental crisis. Today about 2.8 billion people—about 40 percent of the world's population—live in areas with some degree of water scarcity.

Global warming is one thing that is reducing the freshwater supply. Rising temperatures are causing Earth's glaciers to shrink. This is decreasing the water supply that comes from glaciers. For thousands of years, glaciers in the southern Himalayas have helped feed major rivers in South Asia. The rivers provide freshwater for more than 1 billion people. That's nearly a sixth of the world's population. But now these life-giving masses of ice are in danger of disappearing. In addition to the glaciers, a lot of lakes will shrink and disappear as the world's air continues to warm up. For example, Lake Chad in central Africa was once the sixth largest lake in the world. Today it has shrunk to one-twentieth of its former size, and experts expect it to disappear completely in this century. The main reason is a lack of rainfall caused by a warming climate.

The false belief that water will always be readily available has led to many of the world's water problems. Scientists have documented some startling facts about this. For example, badly planned dams are causing reservoirs to lose millions

Lack of rainfall is threatening the water supply for many people in Africa.

Water Use

According to the U.S. Environmental Protection Agency, global water consumption increased sixfold between 1900 and 1995. This is more than double the world's population growth rate. Farming is responsible for 70 percent of this usage, and much of the water used is wasted. Some experts say 50 percent of water used for crops and yards is wasted because of overwatering, evaporation, or being blown away by wind.

of gallons of water through evaporation. Meanwhile, the trickle of water passing through some of these dams is so small that the surrounding wetlands are going dry. For the past century, the world's water use has grown more than twice as fast as its population. This means that rivers, lakes, and the underground waters that supply wells and springs are being drained faster than rain can refill them.

Equally disturbing is the problem of water pollution, most of which is also caused by humans. Every time it rains, poisons from pesticides, fertilizers, and other chemical products flow into the water supply. Sewage and seawater are also finding their way into many freshwater systems, making them unusable. Oil spills frequently turn bodies of water into slick toxic dumps. Everywhere

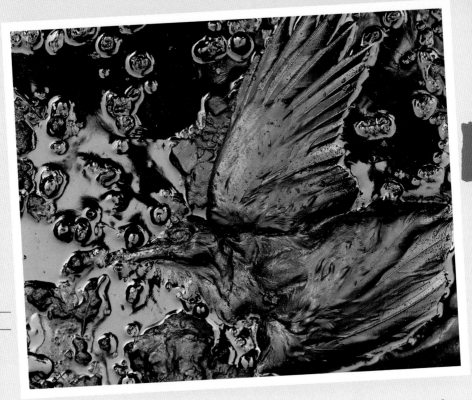

Oil spills kill birds and marine animals and threaten the health of humans as well.

on Earth, people casually dump trash of all kinds into lakes, streams, and oceans every day.

Water pollution doesn't just ruin people's water activities and spoil the beauty of nature. It limits the supply of freshwater and hurts living things. It can lead to serious diseases in humans and, in some cases, even death.

The Clean Water Act:

The Clean Water Act is one of the U.S. government's most important tools for protecting the water within the nation's borders. When the law was passed, in 1972, its purpose was mainly tracking and reducing chemical water pollution. The law focused on common sources of pollution, such

Bringing Life to Lake Erie

Concerned about water pollution? Don't underestimate your ability to make a difference. Your government can help. Here's one example: In the 1960s, Lake Erie, one of the Great Lakes, was considered by environmentalists to be a "dead" lake. Fish and other animals died, and the lake's surface was covered by a smelly scum. Scientists discovered that chemicals called phosphates, which are found in laundry detergents, were making their way into the lake and causing a chain reaction that used up the oxygen in the lake. But in the 1970s, U.S. citizens worked through their government to ban phosphates in laundry detergents. Eventually Lake Erie came back to life.

as sewage systems and factories. But in the 1980s, other causes of pollution began to get attention. The Environmental Protection Agency started monitoring construction sites, urban storm sewer systems, and agricultural activities much more closely. Today those who enforce the law work to preserve healthy waters and to restore waters that have become polluted.

You can help! With so many threats to the planet's water supply, it's a good thing scientists and government watchdogs are on the job. But even if you don't work for the EPA, there are plenty of ways you can help keep our water fresh, clean, and plentiful. According to businessman and politician Ross Perot, "The activist is not the man who says the river is dirty. The activist is

Trash in rivers and lakes threatens the health of all living things.

Gross Violations

The Environmental Protection Agency has a fat file full of records of criminal violations of the environmental protection laws. One example is a case from 2008. The Eco Finishing Company, based in Fridley, Minnesota, was found guilty of criminally violating the Clean Water Act. The company's business of coating metal products was resulting in the dumping of illegal levels of metals and cyanide into the local sewer system. Cyanide is a strong poison that instantly kills people if it is swallowed.

During visits by EPA inspectors, the company reduced the amount of toxins it was discharging to make it look as if no violations were occurring. This was purposeful deception of the government. But an employee of the company reported the violation. The company's president and chief executive officer was found guilty of committing crimes, including two counts of felony violations of the Clean Water Act. He was sentenced to serve 15 months in prison and do 200 hours of community service after his release. He also had to pay a $250,000 fine. A special agent of the EPA's Criminal Investigative Division said, "This sentence should put companies … on notice. We will continue to vigorously prosecute crimes committed against our environment."

GO DEEP

the man who cleans up the river." Here are some ways you can help:

- Turn off the faucet while brushing your teeth and save eight gallons (30 liters) of water every day.
- Don't use the toilet as a wastebasket. Because each flush can use as much as 4.5 gallons (17 liters) of water, don't waste water flushing items that can be simply thrown in the trash.
- Don't flush medicine. When drugs are flushed down the toilet, they can end up in the water

Turning off the water while you're brushing your teeth can save thousands of gallons a year.

people and animals drink. Make sure your family disposes of old pills properly. Many pharmacies recycle unused medicine. Find out whether your pharmacy has a recycling program.

- Take short showers rather than baths, which use much more water.
- Get leaky faucets and showerheads fixed immediately. One drip per second equals approximately 3,000 gallons (11,400 liters) wasted each year.
- Two gallons (7.6 liters) of water are used for each minute the tap is running. If you wash dishes by hand, clean them in a sink full of warm soapy water rather than holding them under a running tap. When all are washed, rinse them together—quickly.
- If you use a dishwasher,

save water and energy by washing only full loads of dishes, and scrape them off rather than rinsing them before putting them in the dishwasher. Similarly, wash only full loads of clothing.

- Chill drinking water in the refrigerator rather than letting tap water run until cold.
- Don't throw any kind of trash, oil, or other non-biodegradable liquid or object into a body of water—or into the gutter. It can harm animals and, when rain comes, it may wash right into a sewer system.

"To forget how to dig the earth and tend the soil is to forget ourselves."
—Mohandas K. Gandhi (1869–1948), Indian political and spiritual leader

The Ground We Plant In

chapter 3

The world needs plentiful, healthy soil if living things are going to grow in it. Without good soil, we'd have a lot fewer delicious things to eat. So the lack of rich, clean soil is another issue to get active about.

The biggest problems are erosion, compaction, nutrient loss, and chemical leaching.

The natural removal of soil by wind and water has been going on for eons. But these days human activity is accelerating erosion to an alarming degree. Deforestation plays a major role. When trees are cut down or burned, there are no longer any living roots to hold

the soil in place, nor any leafy canopies to protect the ground from the effects of rain and wind. Farming that uses heavy, powerful equipment is another cause of erosion. These machines not only erode soil, but they can cause soil compaction, too. The weight of these machines presses the ground down into a hard, solid mass. For a plant's root system to dig down into the ground and absorb nutrients, the soil must be loose. Compacted soil is as hard to penetrate as a clenched fist.

The nutrients that plants need for growth are most often used up by conventional farming. Land preparation and plant cultivation remove nutritious organic matter from the soil. So does burning vegetation to clear land for crops. When the soil nutrients are gone, little plant

Erosion happens when trees are cut down, allowing wind and rain to wash away the soil.

life will grow. This in turn increases erosion.

Many farmers use pesticides to kill insects and weeds that harm their crops. But pesticides sometimes damage more than unwanted pests. The chemicals in artificial pesticides can remain in the soil for many years. They can get into vegetables, fruits, or grains that people eat and make their way into the water supply.

Organic alternatives:

Conventional farms give us lots of wonderful things to eat, but their practices are hard on the soil. Organic farms are a gentler option. Organic farmers grow crops without using chemical pesticides and artificial fertilizers. Instead they use natural methods to improve the soil and discourage pests. They might practice crop rotation, in which a different crop is

Pesticides and chemical fertilizers stay in the soil for many years and can have negative effects on animals.

grown on a piece of land each season in order to keep the soil fertile and discourage pests that damage certain crops. The farmers might create habitats for animals, such as birds, that eat insects that threaten their crops.

Organic farmers also use compost to enrich the soil. Compost is rotting organic matter, such as grass clippings, leaves, and vegetable scraps, that can be used as a fertilizer. Mixed with soil, it releases its nutrients and helps plants grow naturally—and without causing pollution.

Composting yields rich organic material to enrich the soil.

You can help! There are many small things you can do to give back to the soil a little of what's been taken away. Here are a few ideas:

- Plant a tree. You'll help prevent erosion, clean the air, and create wildlife habitat all at the same time.
- Buy organic foods, or grow them yourself. You don't have to worry about being exposed to dangerous chemicals, and many people think organic fruits and vegetables just taste better.
- Compost your vegetable scraps and add the mixture to your garden. Besides helping your garden grow, compost keeps kitchen waste from adding to landfills.

- Instead of fertilizing your lawn with chemicals, leave grass clippings on the lawn when you mow. The clippings are full of nitrogen, which promotes lush, green growth.
- Dispose of hazardous materials properly. Don't put them in landfills, where toxic chemicals might get into the soil.

Recycle With Care

Here are just a few of the many household items that are considered hazardous. Check with your recycling center for the best ways to dispose of them. Don't ever just throw them away!

- motor oil
- leftover paint
- medications
- batteries
- electronic equipment

Check It

> "Is civilization progress? The ... final answer will be given not by our amassing of knowledge, or by the discoveries of our science, or by the speed of our aircraft, but by the effect our civilized activities as a whole have upon the quality of our planet's life—the life of plants and animals as well as that of men."
>
> —Charles A. Lindbergh (1902–1974), aviator, author, and environmentalist

Saving the Forests

chapter 4

Some people still use the term tree-hugger in a not-so-complimentary way when referring to those who care passionately about the living world, especially forests. But it's past time for a planetary push to protect trees and all other life on Earth. If we don't watch it, there soon won't be that much left to hug!

Our breathing forests:

The planet's forests—especially the vast tropical rain forests—have been referred to as Earth's lungs. But unlike human lungs, they take in carbon dioxide and emit oxygen. Trees

are one of the planet's best weapons in the fight against global warming. They clean the air, stabilize the soil, and provide habitat for animals. Trees are crucial to our planet in ways that are too numerous to count. But deforestation is putting our woodlands under increasing stress. Most of this defor- estation is occurring in the world's rain forests, where more than 37 million acres

The world's rain forests contain more species than any other ecosystem on Earth.

(15 million hectares) are destroyed every year. Brazil's rain forests are being hit the hardest. There, between 2000 and 2005, 7.9 million acres (3.1 million hectares) of forest were destroyed each year. From 2005 through 2008, Brazil's Atlantic forest regions suffered a loss nine

Rain forests are being cleared for farming and lumber at an alarming rate.

times as great as in the previous three years. The area cleared during those years equaled the size of almost 1,000 soccer fields!

Unfortunately it's the forests made up of the oldest and largest trees that are mostly being cut down. With only about 20 percent of old-growth forests left in the world, the state of our planet's woodlands is critical. Our lives depend in part on the oxygen generated by these biologically complex forests. They give us plants that are invaluable in a multitude of ways. And of course they also support the lives of many kinds of animals.

Most deforestation occurs to make room for farms,

to get lumber for fuel, or to satisfy the world's huge appetite for wood products. Companies that log these forests point out that they often put tree farms in the bare areas. According to a United Nations study, 57 wealthy nations reported that their areas of forest cover actually grew between 2000 and 2005. The problem is that the replacement trees that are planted usually belong to a single species. This sacrifices biological diversity, which is important for making an environment healthy. In other words, tree farms don't make a forest.

The rich complexity of life contained in old-growth

Farming is one of the main causes of rain forest destruction.

The Amazing Rain Forest

20%   The amount of Earth's oxygen that scientists estimate is produced in the Amazon rain forest

30%   The percentage of Earth's forests that have been destroyed in the past 200 years

700   The number of tree species contained in a single 25-acre (10-hectare) plot of rain forest on the island of Borneo—a number equal to the total number of tree species in North America

Less than 1%   The percentage of rain forest species studied by scientists for their active components or possible uses

70%   The percentage of plants with anti-cancer properties that are found only in the rain forest

50,000   The number of plant and animal species believed to be lost each year because of rain forest destruction

forests doesn't spring up overnight. It takes countless decades for a forest full of giant trees and varied species to develop. When all this is wiped out, we lose plants and animals we know about, as well as untold numbers of species we haven't even discovered. One of the most critical losses is of plants that might hold cures for diseases. Tree farms will never adequately make up for old-growth deforestation. The bottom line is this: The world needs these forests, and everything must be done to protect what's left of them.

You can help!

Small efforts or changes you make to your lifestyle can help prevent deforestation and its effects. Here are some easy ways to help:

- Some companies destroy rain forests to grow orange trees, especially in Brazil. If you drink packaged orange juice, be sure the container label says it comes from U.S.-grown oranges.

Ten Foods First Found in the Rain Forest

- bananas
- oranges
- lemons
- peanuts
- cocoa
- eggplant
- avocados
- coconuts
- vanilla
- sugar

- Plant a tree. There may not be deforestation in your area, but it's definitely happening. Any tree—anywhere—can remove carbon dioxide from the air and slow global warming.

- Try to eat nuts and dried fruits whose package labels say they come from "sustainably harvested rain forests." This means they were grown in ways that don't damage the rain forests or any living thing in them.

President Barack Obama helped plant a tree at an event organized by the Student Conservation Association.

Save the Trees

When Hannah McHardy moved to Seattle, Washington, from Arkansas, she fell in love with the forests of the Pacific Northwest. When she discovered that logging was destroying the old-growth forests that had become so important to her, she began working hard to educate people about forestland destruction and how to take action against it. In 2004 her efforts won her the Brower Youth Award and $3,000 from the Earth Island Institute. This annual award honors young people who show outstanding leadership in projects that promote environmental conservation, preservation, or restoration.

"With the rapid rate our planet is being destroyed," Hannah says, "we are the last generation that will have the choice of wilderness, clean air, abundant wildlife, and ancient forests unless something is done. ... It is up to the youth to keep the movement innovative, effective, fresh, and most importantly FUN! Just go out and make yourself heard!"

• Cut down on beef in your diet. Every year thousands of acres of rain forest are destroyed to make grazing pastures for cattle. For every single quarter-pound fast-food hamburger you eat that comes from rain forest cattle (and most ground beef does), a forested area the size of a small kitchen (about 55 square feet, or nearly 5 square meters) is destroyed.

- Half of all felled trees end up as paper—so use less! Take a canvas bag to the store to carry home your purchases. Use both sides of printer paper, and recycle it when you're finished. Avoid using paper cups and plates.

- Ask your parents not to buy products made from endangered rain forest trees. These include teak, ebony, rosewood, and mahogany. The wood is beautiful, but logging companies are bringing these trees close to extinction because of consumer demand.

A logger seems small next to an old-growth tree he has felled.

> "*If all the beasts were gone, men would die from a great loneliness of spirit, for whatever happens to the beasts also happens to the man. All things are connected. Whatever befalls the Earth befalls the sons of the Earth.*"
> —Chief Seattle (c. 1786-1866), Native American leader

Animals in Danger

chapter 5

All the threads that make up Earth's rich tapestry are interconnected. When air is polluted, it affects the water. When water becomes polluted, it affects the plants that depend on it for nourishment. So it's only natural that deforestation, global warming, and other environmental problems are putting animals at risk. According to the International Union for Conservation of Nature, 99 percent of all species are endangered by human activity. Another report predicts the extinction of a full 25 percent of all plant and vertebrate

Wildlife in Africa is becoming increasingly threatened by nearby human activity.

animal species by 2050. There are many success stories about bringing living things back from the edge of permanent disappearance. Yet many remain on the list of endangered or threatened species, and often new ones are added.

One of these is the polar bear, the world's largest carnivorous mammal. In May 2008, the U.S. Department of the Interior added the polar bear to the list as a threatened species. Since many politicians favor massive oil and gas development where polar bears live, this is a positive step.

It's also a seemingly necessary step. Scientists at the U.S. Geological Survey believe that by 2050 at least two-thirds of the world's polar bears could be wiped out because of global warming. This would include all of Alaska's big white bears.

Records show that, in general, global warming is causing Arctic sea ice to melt a little earlier each summer. This makes it more challenging for polar bears to hunt for prey, so it's difficult for them to gain the weight they need to get through the winter without food. The cubs born in the spring are lighter and less healthy. It's harder for smaller, thinner cubs to survive in their harsh habitat. The decrease in sea ice also makes polar bears have to swim much farther. Scientists have reported stranded or drowning polar bears, something they had not seen until recently.

Polar bears will be at risk of extinction because of habitat destruction if global warming continues.

The Encyclopedia of Life

One of the most interesting conservation projects today is the Encyclopedia of Life. The EOL is an online database that someday could include all forms of life known on Earth.

Leading this vast, visionary project of information-gathering is E.O. Wilson, a biologist at Harvard University. His aim is to collect every known bit of information about every living thing. This ranges from the largest mammals on Earth right down to organisms so small they're invisible to the naked eye. Each species will have its own Web site, which will be continually updated as new information is gathered.

The purpose of this project is to help save the planet. EOL's coordinators believe that having a source of "central intelligence" will aid in the effort to understand the planet's problems and decide how to fix them.

It makes sense. Humans have identified about 1.8 million organisms, but scientists estimate that

As animal habitats shrink or are destroyed by global warming or human development, more alarming reports are coming to light. Orangutans are being killed or pushed out of their homelands as palm oil plantations are created, destroying their habitat.

Coral reefs are dying because of global warming, destroying habitat for hundreds of thousands of marine species. Overfishing, pollution, and global warming threaten to deplete the world's fisheries by the middle of this century. And this is just some of the bad news.

this is only 10 percent of all living things on Earth. Discovering the other 90 percent, Wilson says, will be made much easier by having the collective knowledge about all known organisms in one database. And with the discovery of previously unknown living things, new possibilities appear. Perhaps some of the undiscovered species hold the key to curing diseases or solving other critical problems we deal with today.

The EOL isn't just for scientists. Anyone can access the database. In the same spirit of sharing, anyone will be able to add to this giant "map of biodiversity." Scientists and nonscientists alike can contribute information, which will be checked for accuracy by experts. The EOL encourages students and even whole classes to sign up and get involved. If you are looking for a class project, the EOL may be a great starting place.

Poaching for profit:

One of the greatest worldwide threats to wildlife is poaching, which means illegally capturing or killing endangered animals. The sale of wildlife around the world brings in billions of black-market dollars. People want animals for their skin, fur, tusks, and meat. Whatever the reason, the criminals profit while the world's wildlife population is rapidly being diminished.

In many poor, rural regions of the world, poaching is motivated by the need to survive. Often people in these areas find it difficult

The poaching of elephant tusks puts an
already endangered species at greater risk.

to balance the need to
preserve wildlife habitat
with their own need to make
a living. On the upside,
many worldwide animal-
protection organizations
are educating people and
helping them find other
ways to sustain themselves.
The movement to protect
animals of every kind, from
polar bears to the tiniest

bugs on Earth, has become
increasingly important all
around the world.

The Endangered Species Act:
One U.S.
law helping to fight the
decline of certain wildlife
populations, no matter the
reason, is the Endangered
Species Act. The law, passed
in 1973, is considered one

of the most successful laws on the books. It established the list of endangered and threatened species and prohibits the unauthorized taking, possession, sale, or transporting of these species. There are penalties for violations of the law and rewards for people who give information that helps catch and punish violators. One of its most important effects is protecting the ecosystems where America's threatened and endangered species live.

You can help! When most people hear "endangered species," they think of manatees, polar bears, whales, and other large, exciting animals. If these creatures don't live in your area, you might think there is nothing you can do to help. But the endangered species list contains nearly 1,300 plants, birds, fish, mammals, and other species. You're likely

Comeback Kids

Thanks to human efforts, 10 species that were once almost extinct are now no longer in danger:

- American alligator
- gray wolf
- blue poison frog
- grizzly bear
- koala
- black-footed ferret
- California condor
- bison
- bald eagle
- African white rhinoceros

Check It

to find some animal that lives in or migrates through your area. People play a critical role in protecting our country's wildlife and plants. Here are some ways you can be an activist:

• "Adopt" an endangered species native to your area. Find out how you can help protect it, and tell people in your community about your adopted plant or animal. You could make a Web page, write a newspaper article, give a speech, distribute brochures, or do whatever else you can think of.

Talk with your neighbors, and encourage them to get involved in environmental causes.

Cars are a hazard for many animals, so watch the road!

• When your family is driving in areas where animals may be present, slow down and look out for wildlife. Collisions with cars and trucks are a major problem in certain areas for many endangered species, such as Florida black bears, Florida panthers, desert tortoises, Key deer, indigo snakes, and Houston toads. About 65 percent of Florida panther and Florida black bear deaths are related to highway accidents.

Turn your backyard into a wildlife habitat. You can learn a lot about animals by watching them up close.

- If you see evidence that people have killed wildlife illegally, contact your state's fish and game department. State agencies handle violations of state wildlife laws and deal with most local wildlife management problems.
- Don't buy products that come from endangered or threatened plant and animal species.
- Make your backyard wildlife-friendly. Plant native trees and bushes with berries or nuts that provide birds and other creatures with food and a place to live.

Monkey Business

Janine Licare and Aislin Livingstone were concerned about the number of monkeys killed by cars when trying to cross the road near their home in Manuel Antonio, Costa Rica. They sold painted rocks and used the money they made to build monkey bridges. These bridges—a series of wires high above the roadways—allow monkeys to cross the road well above traffic, keeping them out of harm's way. The pair's success prompted them to found Kids Saving the Rainforest, an organization aimed at preserving local rain forest land, rehabilitating baby and injured animals, creating a wildlife sanctuary for animals that can't be released into the wild, and educating children about the rain forest and the many animals that make it their home.

"You don't have to be a lawmaker, scientist, or in the White House to take action to protect the environment. Reduce your own impact on the environment in your daily lives. Most importantly, get educated."
—Leonardo DiCaprio, actor and environmental activist

Looking to the Future

chapter 6

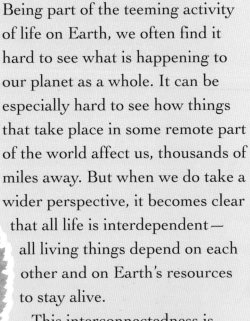

Being part of the teeming activity of life on Earth, we often find it hard to see what is happening to our planet as a whole. It can be especially hard to see how things that take place in some remote part of the world affect us, thousands of miles away. But when we do take a wider perspective, it becomes clear that all life is interdependent — all living things depend on each other and on Earth's resources to stay alive.

This interconnectedness is complex. It means that when something breaks down in the environment somewhere, the effect ripples outward around the globe. Eventually all living things feel the consequences, to a greater or lesser degree. With assaults against the environment occurring on nearly every front, the efforts to reverse things must be a global undertaking. And there's no time to waste — the clock is ticking.

Urgent matters: As it turns out, not every negative effect can be reversed. In January 2009, the National Academy of Sciences reported that some global warming is already irreversible. "This is really a wakeup call about the seriousness of this issue," said Princeton University geoscientist Jorge

Global warming is limiting many animals' access to water.

Sarmiento. Indeed it is.

On a positive note, though, millions have already responded to this wakeup call. Awareness of the world's urgent environmental problems has never been greater. And the technologies available to fix much of what's wrong have never been more advanced. Clean, renewable energy can be made using the sun, wind, water, plants, and Earth's internal heat. These types of energy are becoming increasingly available and affordable. Reducing or eliminating our need for fossil fuels is the most important thing we can do to stop global warming and preserve the abundant life on Earth.

Wind turbines convert the movement of air—a clean, renewable resource—into electrical power.

Ten Earth-Focused Groups

- Global Green
  http://globalgreen.org
- Greenbelt Movement
  www.greenbeltmovement.org
- Greenpeace International
  www.greenpeace.org
- National Wildlife Federation
  www.nwf.org
- Natural Resources Defense Council
  www.nrdc.org
- Rainforest Action Network
  http://ran.org
- Sierra Club
  www.sierraclub.org
- Windstar Foundation
  www.wstar.org
- World Environmental Organization
  www.world.org
- World Wildlife Fund
  www.worldwildlife.org

Protecting the Planet

Saving the blue marble:

Renewable energy is vital in preserving our planet's future, but there's another renewable resource that has even broader promise. As Al Gore, the environmental activist, Nobel Prize winner, and former vice president, has said, "The will to act is a renewable resource." Humanity really can stop the destruction. If we all pitch in, much can be done to save planet Earth, our beautiful blue marble, so that

↑ Working with others to protect the environment increases both your effectiveness and your enjoyment.

it remains a vibrant habitat for all living things. It is time for everyone to become an environmental activist. Simple steps you take today will help to preserve the air, water, soil, trees, and animals for generations to come. Together we can become a force for change. What will you do to help?

Glossary

biodiversity—variety of species of plants and animals in an environment

carbon dioxide—greenhouse gas most responsible for global warming

compost—mixture of decayed organic material that is used for fertilizing

deforestation—action or process of clearing forests

fertilizers—substances, such as manure or chemicals, used to make soil richer and better for growing crops

fossil fuels—fuels, including coal, oil, and natural gas, made from the remains of ancient organisms

global warming—rise in the average worldwide temperature of Earth's atmosphere

greenhouse gases—gases in a planet's atmosphere that trap energy from the sun

ozone layer—layer of the upper atmosphere that absorbs harmful ultraviolet light

natural resources—substances found in nature that people use, such as soil, air, trees, coal, and oil; some are renewable, while others have a fixed supply

non-biodegradable—unable to decay and be absorbed by the environment

organic—grown without the use of chemical fertilizers, pesticides, or other artificial substances

pesticides—substances, usually chemical, applied to crops to kill harmful insects and other pests

smog—haze caused by pollution

Investigate Further

MORE BOOKS TO READ

Amsel, Sheri. *The Everything Kids' Environment Book*. Avon, Mass.: Adams Media, 2007.

Coley, Mary McIntyre. *Environmentalism: How You Can Make a Difference*. Mankato, Minn.: Capstone Press, 2009.

Hall, Julie. *A Hot Planet Needs Cool Kids*. Bainbridge Island, Wash.: Green Goat Books, 2007.

Thornhill, Jan. *This Is My Planet: The Kids' Guide to Global Warming*. Toronto: Maple Tree Press, 2007.

INTERNET SITES

FactHound offers a safe, fun way to find Internet sites related to this book. All of the sites on FactHound have been researched by our staff.

Here's all you do:
    Visit *www.facthound.com*
FactHound will fetch the best sites for you!

Index

About the Author

Pamela Dell began her professional career writing for adults and started writing for young readers about 12 years ago. Since then she has written fiction and nonfiction books, written numerous magazine articles, and created award-winning interactive multimedia.